SURVIVE ADULTERY WHILE IN MARRIAGE

How To Survive Adultery While In Marriage

Contents

INTRODUCTION

Your wedding day has finally arrived, and it was the kind of courtship that only Cinderella could have dreamed of having. It is the day you have been preparing for since you were young and finally arrived. As you expect the doors to open and begin to take those first steps down the aisle, the feeling of completion in your heart is palpable. Your dream man is waiting for you at the end of the aisle, and as soon as the vows have been exchanged, the start of your happily ever after will finally be here.

When we think of getting married, this is the image that comes to mind. We tend to forget that the marriage's actual beginning doesn't occur until after the honeymoon has ended. To preserve and strengthen your marriage, you will need to put in a lot of effort during that first year and the years to come. However, what results from the presence of infidelity in the relationship? Does it necessarily mean that you will no longer be married?

FORMS OF ADULTERY

Most acts of adultery are not planned yet; 30% to 60% of men and women will cheat on their spouses. Adultery is usually situationally driven.

In couples, emotional infidelity can occur when one partner feels unheard or when their spouse is just absent from the home. This may lead to you or your partner confiding in a buddy of the other sex. Outside your marriage, intimate facts of your relationship are being discussed, and you might start spending more time with the "other" person.

There is no sexual component to the connection in this instance. In addition to discussing private topics with someone other than your husband, adultery also involves creating an environment where a sexual act may occur.

Looking at others with a lusty glance is a form of visual adultery. When your relationship loses intimacy, this may occur. Your carnal desires override your desire for sex because it isn't happening. When something or someone appeals to our eyes, we glance at them. We seek elsewhere when our marriages have started to make us uncomfortable. Whatever its appearance, adultery is an act that slashes our innermost souls. It is an agony that has no words to express it.

EXAMPLES OF ADULTEROUS RELATIONSHIPS IN THE BIBLE

The maxim "if it feels good, it's acceptable" has gained acceptance in today's society. This is nothing new, as Christians are aware. The Bible is full of instances of adulterous partnerships.

An Old Testament illustration of an adulterous relationship is that of Hosea and Gomer. Gomer, a notoriously promiscuous lady, was to be Hosea's bride. Hosea and Gomer got married and had kids together. Gomer divorces her husband to continue having relationships with other men, with whom she later had children.

Go, demonstrate your love to your wife again; the Lord commands Hosea despite Gomer's immoral actions. They make up when Hosea pays her fifteen shekels to buy her back.

Later on, we read about an unfaithful lady who was caught in the act in the book of John. The Pharisees and professors of the law bring her to the Temple. Numerous people have gathered to hear Jesus speak while he is in the Temple. The Pharisees utilized this as an opportunity to catch Jesus off guard by asking him what he would do. Anyone who is sinless should cast the first stone, he responds. Jesus advises her to leave her sinful life and does not judge her for it.

These two accounts are examples of how wrong adultery is, but that forgiveness is possible.

HOW IS FORGIVENESS POSSIBLE AFTER ADULTERY?

The most challenging thing to give someone who has deeply wounded you is forgiveness. Only with God's aid is it possible for humans to forgive.

You or your spouse may receive God's unqualified forgiveness. The Lord says, "Come on, let's settle this now," in the words of the prophet Isaiah. Although your sins are red like crimson, they will be like wool; though they are like scarlet, they will be white as snow. These are our words of hope. They remind us that forgiveness is possible and necessary in our connection with Christ.

If your brothers or sisters transgress against you, correct them; if they repent, forgive them, Jesus says in Luke 17:3. This is the commandment we have to provide forgiveness to those who have wronged us. I cannot dispute that some marriages will end due to adultery. I can tell that forgiveness is possible, whether you want to stay married or get a divorce.

HOW CAN YOUR MARRIAGE OVERCOME ADULTERY?

When you have felt the pain that comes with adultery, it isn't easy to believe that your marriage would ever work. I advise you to think about the following aspects and queries of your relationship before giving up:

1. At one point, was your relationship healthy?

You must consider the period before the adultery to respond to this question. You might think back on the enjoyable occasions during this period. You may browse through pictures or souvenirs from memorable experiences or list the fun times you shared.

2. Is your spouse prepared to be open and honest about what transpired?

It isn't easy to process details of adulterous behavior, but you need to know that your partner will provide them upon request. You must have faith that your partner will be receptive to their feelings. Your partner must be willing to take the time to think about their actions and share their feelings with you.

3. Should you regain faith in your spouse, will you remarry them?

You'll need to consider who your spouse is to answer this question. Are they trustworthy people who erred? You should reflect on why you fell in love and wanted to spend your life with that person.

4. Are you and your partner ready to renegotiate the parameters of your union?

You and your husband must decide if you're ready to start over after reflecting on your relationship before adultery. Are you prepared to reconsider and renegotiate terms so that you can advance and forge a bond that is stronger than ever?

God created marriage as a lovely act. Adultery is a possibility in marriage because the parties involved are immoral. If adultery mars your marriage, there is still hope that it won't spell the end of your union.

We can be forgiven by God and our spouses, as shown by the biblical instances of Hosea, Gomer, and the adulterous woman. We have the chance to restore our marriages and put Christ where he belongs, at the center, if we confess our sin and turn from it.

RECOGNIZE ADULTERY AS A SIN

Proverbs 6:32 puts it best: "But whoso commits adultery with a woman lacks sense; he who does it destroys his soul." Therein lies the core of what sin is—self-destruction.

God doesn't establish His regulations to stifle our freedom or prevent us from having fun. His every command stems from an eternal love for people and an eternal perspective that sees all things through to their conclusion. God is aware that some actions harm us, if not now, then in the future. These actions fall under the category of sin.

Since adultery is one of the Ten Commandments and is referenced frequently in the Bible, it seems to retain a special place among all sins. However, this isn't because one sin is worse than another in

God's eyes; instead, adultery causes a particular form of ruin in the human heart.

Consider this. Your spouse is meant to be your safe haven. He is your refuge, the one person in the entire world you may have the utmost faith in. That's why being deceived by your spouse is something you may not fully recover from for years. God condemns adultery because of this. When we abandon our vows, we turn what is God's gift into a nightmare. Marriage is supposed to be the ideal haven.

KNOW THAT YOU CAN LEAVE

In Malachi 2:16, God boldly says, "I hate divorce." No matter what your husband did wrong, it would appear that this would automatically end any thoughts of divorce.

Contrary to general belief, the Bible does not mandate that you remain with an unfaithful spouse. Simply said, this is untrue.

Let's examine what is spoken in the Bible.

In Matthew 19:9, Jesus says, "whoever divorces his wife, except on the grounds of sexual immorality, and marries another commits adultery." You'll notice the word "except"—if your partner engages in sexual adultery, you are not required by Scripture to remain in a relationship with them.

In 1 Corinthians 7:15, Paul also writes, "if the unbelieving partner depart, let him leave. A sister or a brother is not under slavery in such cases. God has called you to peace."

You are not a prisoner to a partner who repeatedly betrays, deserts, or mistreats you. God does allow divorce in these situations because He wants you to live a peaceful life. However, as we're about to discover, God wants you to at least try to mend your marriage if your cheating spouse is willing to change.

RECOGNIZE THE MEANING OF FORGIVENESS

It is preferable if you can get the fortitude to forgive a cheating spouse and determine precisely what went wrong when they repent. Before you proceed, let's first discuss what forgiveness is and, more importantly, what it isn't.

Generally speaking, forgiveness is letting go of the urge for retaliation and retribution, which is incredibly challenging when you've been duped. Despite the unbelievable betrayal, forgiveness enables the forgiver to find serenity.

If possible, Paul advises us to make up with our spouse in 1 Corinthians 7:10–11. God is aware that occasionally even morally upright individuals make mistakes. A relationship can recover after an affair, figure out why it took place, and emerge stronger than before.

God prefers this outcome over the lifetime of suffering and guilt that results from breaking off the relationship. Marriages are healed by forgiveness.

REALIZE WHAT FORGIVENESS ISN'T

Although God desires that we forgive, He does not, as we have already stated, desire that we injure ourselves by continuing to be with someone who does not value us.

Permitting behavior is not forgiveness. Forgiving someone does not include continuing to overlook their repeated betrayals of trust by your spouse. It does not imply that you should act as though the affair is not taking place. It also means that you consent to be exploited by your spouse.

No, you should leave if your partner cheats frequently. It is preferable to choose to heal, if possible, if they are sorry and prepared to put some effort into making better decisions, forgiving, and reconciling. However, find someone else if your partner doesn't value you highly enough to quit harming you. Being forgiven is not meant to turn you into a doormat.

PRAY FOR RECOVERY

Speaking to God can be one of the wondrous things you can do if you've discovered that your spouse cheated on you. It's easy to disregard the power of prayer, especially in trying circumstances.

You can quickly move away and express your sentiments by praying. Just offer God everything, including your rage and pain. You won't insult Him, I assure you. Tell Him how you're feeling. After venting, start praying for the future. Pray that your spouse will be able to forgive you and that their heart will be made righteous once more. This can prevent you from consistently dwelling on the bad and encouraging God to act in your life.

Finally, ask God to use your suffering for good somehow. Praying for an open mind is essential because grief may teach us things that few other experiences can. Sometimes praying produces results; conversing with God aids in our ability to maintain our attention on his purposes for our life. Make time for God if you find yourself in this tremendously challenging situation. You won't be sorry.

MOVING ON

When addressing infidelity, the Bible paints a picture of a challenging path. Although God allows divorce when a partner betrays or deserts you, He prefers to see forgiveness and reconciliation because they are best for us in the long run.

So bear these spiritual truths in mind when you go to counseling and attempt to fix your marriage. Don't feel confined to a life of suffering, but don't give up on the notion of peace either. Your partnership might emerge from this test stronger than ever. The following bible texts and explanations would help you more.

Proverbs 3: 5-6 says, "Trust in the Lord with all thine heart, and lean not unto thine own understanding. In all thy ways, accept him, and he shall direct thy paths."

Whether you've experienced betrayal before, living in an adulterous relationship can make you feel as though no one else can comprehend how upset you are. No matter how awful someone else's experience may have been, being betrayed makes you feel alone, and your experience feels worse. Turn to your Lord and Savior for help and direction rather than listening to others on the outside trying to advise you how to handle your partner's infidelity. Tell Him about your worries and frustrations in conversation. You will find comfort in the route He directs you towards, even though He may not speak to you personally.

1 Corinthians 7:15-17 says

"But if the unbeliever departs, let him depart; a brother or sister is not under bondage in such cases. But God has called us to peace. For what knowest thou, O wife, whether thou shalt save thy husband? Or how knowest thou, O man, whether thou shalt save thy wife? But as God has distributed to every man, as the Lord has called everyone, so let him walk."

You can't control your husband since life happens. Even if you have a close bond, the other person might not. Embrace that. Recognize that each person has a unique existence and a unique destiny. Though you may experience disappointments and roadblocks along the path, remember that God is with you every step of the way. Don't ask God why He would subject you to suffering because of this adulterous relationship. Don't hold Him accountable for your partner's adultery. And don't let your partner's lack of judgment lead the rest of your world to collapse. Instead, rely on your Lord and Savior and give the reins to Him. He will point you in the direction of your life's purpose. He will show you how to go ahead if it involves forgiving your partner. He will lead you in that direction if that means ending the relationship. Jesus Christ will never abandon you.

Philippians 4: 19.

"But my God shall supply all your needs according to his riches in glory in Christ Jesus."

Seeing the light at the border of the tunnel might be challenging when your life seems to be falling apart, and your heart is in a million pieces. Do not waste time trying to figure out why infidelity destroyed your relationship. Spend less time criticizing yourself and wondering what is wrong with you. Instead, hold your head high and face the world, knowing God will provide everything you need to overcome your unfaithfulness. He is aware of your survival needs. He knows what will make you feel whole once again. Be patient and have faith in what He is doing. Try to hold onto the idea that everything does happen for a purpose in your hindsight.

Isaiah 30: 20-21

"And though the Lord give you the bread of adversity, and the water of affliction, Yet shall not thy teachers be removed into a corner anymore,

But thine eyes shall see thy teachers: And thine ears shall hear a word behind thee, saying, This is the way, walk ye in it, when ye turn to the right hand, and when ye turn to the left.."

Many people dealing with infidelity find it challenging to see the broader picture. Even though they know their God will lead them, their pain overwhelms them and makes them feel helpless. It's crucial to remember that God places people in other people's lives for a reason. Everyone we relate with, whether they are our closest friends, relatives, or strangers, serves a purpose in our lives. Even if God might not be speaking to you when you express your dissatisfaction, it's crucial to realize that He is communicating to you since His voice is much louder and audible throughout your life. When you're feeling lonely and alone, take a moment to glance around and be grateful.

Make sure to keep in mind that you are not alone in this turbulent chaos during this trying period. The act of infidelity that your partner committed affects more than just you. Be aware that while your heart may be broken, bad deeds also significantly impact the world around you. Because of the infidelity, your children, relatives, and friends will all experience tremors and waves. Don't let your sorrow prevent you from being present for those who will need you; together, you can rely on your Lord and Savior for solace and courage. You'll never be alone if you have God!

Life and relationships are not simple affairs. There are happy moments and unhappy times. It's critical to keep in mind that Jesus Christ, your Lord and Savior, is constantly on your side. He has established your framework. Remember that this act of adultery won't break you; if you cooperate with God, it will strengthen you, even though you may not be able to see the broader picture at first.

www.ingramcontent.com/pod-product-compliance
Lightning Source LLC
LaVergne TN
LVHW052114160826
845678LV00015B/3551

* 9 7 9 8 3 5 1 9 8 2 5 2 6 *